Endorsement

"Christians are pressed by very real questions. How does Scripture structure a church, order worship, organize ministry, and define biblical leadership? Those are just examples of the questions that are answered clearly, carefully, and winsomely in this new series from 9Marks. I am so thankful for this ministry and for its incredibly healthy and hopeful influence in so many faithful churches. I eagerly commend this series."

R. Albert Mohler Jr., President, The Southern Baptist Theological Seminary

"Sincere questions deserve thoughtful answers. If you're not sure where to start in answering these questions, let this series serve as a diving board into the pool. These minibooks are winsomely to-the-point and great to read together with one friend or one hundred friends."

Gloria Furman, author, *Missional Motherhood* and *The Pastor's Wife*

"As a pastor, I get asked lots of questions. I'm approached by unbelievers seeking to understand the gospel, new believers unsure about next steps, and maturing believers wanting help answering questions from their Christian family, friends, neighbors, or coworkers. It's in these moments that I wish I had a book to give them that was brief, answered their questions, and pointed them in the right direction for further study. Church Questions is a series that provides just that. Each booklet tackles one question in a biblical, brief, and practical manner. The series may be called Church Questions, but it could be called 'Church Answers.' I intend to pick these up by the dozens and give them away regularly. You should too."

Juan R. Sanchez, Senior Pastor, High Pointe Baptist Church, Austin, Texas

"Where can we Christians find reliable answers to our common questions about life together at church—without having to plow through long, expensive books? The Church Questions booklets meet our need with answers that are biblical, thoughtful, and practical. For pastors, this series will prove a trustworthy resource for guiding church members toward deeper wisdom and stronger unity."

Ray Ortlund, President, Renewal Ministries

How Can I Support International Missions?

Church Questions

How Can I Support International Missions?

Mark Collins

WHEATON, ILLINOIS

Trade paperback ISBN: 978-1-4335-7231-9
ePub ISBN: 978-1-4335-7234-0
PDF ISBN: 978-1-4335-7232-6
Mobipocket ISBN: 978-1-4335-7233-3

Library of Congress Cataloging-in-Publication Data

Names: Collins, Mark, 1973- author.
Title: How can I support international missions? / Mark Collins.
Description: Wheaton, Illinois : Crossway, [2021] | Series: Church questions | Includes index.
Identifiers: LCCN 2021000904 (print) | LCCN 2021000905 (ebook) | ISBN 9781433572319 (trade paperback) | ISBN 9781433572326 (pdf) | ISBN 9781433572333 (mobi) | ISBN 9781433572340 (epub)
Subjects: LCSH: Missions.
Classification: LCC BV2063 .C5835 2021 (print) | LCC BV2063 (ebook) | DDC 266/.023—dc23
LC record available at https://lccn.loc.gov/2021000904
LC ebook record available at https://lccn.loc.gov/2021000905

Crossway is a publishing ministry of Good News Publishers.

BP		30	29	28	27	26	25	24	23	22	21
15	14	13	12	11	10	9	8	7	6	5	4	3	2	1

May God be gracious to us and bless us
and make his face to shine upon us,
Selah
that your way may be known on earth,
your saving power among all nations.

Psalm 67:1–2

Bob and Maxine joined their church in the 1950s as young Christians. They made the church their life. They regularly attended Sunday morning services as well as prayer meetings, and they were consistently involved with the church community throughout the week. Somewhere along the way, they took it upon themselves to get to know the missionaries their church supported. Years later, when my wife and I began to receive support from their church, they wanted to be sure to get our prayer letter. Every furlough we were home, they invited us to dinner. As we talked, they would ask the kind of questions that indicated they had read our letters and had been praying for us. When we had financial needs, they rallied their small group to take up a collection for us. In every way they could, Bob and Maxine showed us that they were behind our work and were with us. Bob went home to be with the Lord a few years ago, but Maxine is still there, still praying for us—we are sure of that.[1]

My goal in this book is to convince you that every Christian should support international missions and also to show you how to do that from wherever God has placed you. I want you to make a habit of supporting missions for the rest of your life. Not every Christian needs to "go" to be faithful, but we're all called to engage in the church's mission to reach the nations together. We all have a role to play.

I didn't always realize this.

As a young Christian, I read missionary biographies like *Shadow of the Almighty*. Jim Elliot and four other missionaries lost their lives on January 8, 1956, at the hands of men from an unreached, remote tribe in Ecuador. Jim Elliot's quote, "He is no fool who gives what he cannot keep to gain what he cannot lose," took on all the more power in my mind because of the way he had lived and died at the age of twenty-eight.[2]

The legacy of missionaries and martyrs like Jim Elliot is a blessing to all Christians. But I sometimes wonder if Christians wrongly infer from these stories that the gospel only spreads across the world in these dramatic ways. Perhaps you have thought to yourself, *My life has nothing dramatic in it. I'm more or less "stuck" in the same place, at the same church, doing many of the same things I was years ago. In fact, I've been doing the same things for the last decade! I must be in a different category of Christian from those who have a great impact for the kingdom.*

Have you ever thought something like that? Well here's some good news: you shouldn't. We shouldn't ever compare our lives with others. God has given each of us our own roles and responsibilities in the church. We shouldn't measure our faithfulness to Christ by how *dramatic* our life and ministry looks.

I don't know what the Lord has in store for your life. God might be moving some of you reading this book to leave the comforts of home to spend your life some place far away laboring for the gospel. My hunch, however, is that God is calling most of you reading this book to something else—something just as worthwhile and significant. Maybe, like Bob and Maxine, God's calling you to recognize the responsibility every Christian has to support missions. I'm writing this book mainly for those people. Christians who aren't going to be vocational missionaries still have a role to play in spreading the good news of Jesus Christ.

Before we talk about how each Christian can support the work of international missions, I'll take the next few pages to make sure we understand a biblical perspective on missions and exactly what the Lord wants his people to do.

Commissioned by Christ to Reach the World

Many passages in Scripture speak to the missionary task, but at the foundation we need to remember that we do missions because Jesus commissioned his people to carry the gospel to the ends of the earth. Two passages in Scripture make this point unmistakably: John 20:21 and Matthew 28:18–20.

"As the Father Has Sent Me,
Even So I Am Sending You" (John 20:21)

The disciples were surely in shock—the man they had seen crucified was standing *alive* before their eyes. John 20 tells us that while barricaded in a hidden room, wondering if a knock at the door might lead to their arrests and executions, Jesus appeared to the disciples showing them the wounds in his hands and his side (John 20:19–29).

Can you imagine how their thoughts would have been racing? *What could it all mean?* Surely nothing would ever be the same.

Consider what Jesus might have said to them in this moment. He could have declared his sovereign power over heaven and earth. He could have explained how the Old Testament had been fulfilled in him. He could have given them more instruction about the kingdom of

God. Instead he chose to tell them two things:
(1) "Peace be with you," and (2) "As the Father
has sent me, even so I am sending you" (John
20:21).

Jesus pronounces peace on the apostles because through his death and resurrection, we
have peace with God. Those who believe the
gospel know the peace that passes all understanding—the peace of a reconciled relationship
with God (Phil. 4:7). No better news exists for
the apostles or for us.

But notice, Jesus doesn't stop with this word
of peace. Instead, the gospel of peace has immediate implications for the apostles: "As the
Father has sent me, even so I am sending you"
(John 20:21). What you do comes from who you
are. Jesus hits both identity and mission in one
sentence. Those two things are one for a disciple
of Jesus. As the Father sent Jesus on a ministry of
mercy to the world, so Jesus sends his disciples
as ministers of mercy.

If you call yourself a Christian, then this is
part of your identity too. Disciples are like their
masters. When we say that we are disciples of

Jesus, we mean that we are his followers—those who recognize him as our teacher, our example, and our Lord. When he sends us on a mission that he first modeled for us, we need to accept that mission as our own. We need to make it our goal to know and pursue the mission for which he sends us. It is a worthy goal!

"Make Disciples of All Nations" (Matt. 28:18–20)

Throughout the Gospels, Jesus always seems to give his disciples more than they bargain for.

In Matthew 28, Matthew records that the group, reeling in shock and awe over his resurrection, had an unsettled mix of emotions: "And when they saw him they worshiped him, *but some doubted*" (Matt. 28:17). Perhaps Jesus will deal with the doubts before he proceeds to their mission? Nope, Jesus simply reminds them of his own sufficiency, glory, and authority. He draws their eyes to his ultimate regency over creation before commissioning them to take the gospel to all the nations :

And Jesus came and said to them, "All authority in heaven and on earth has been given to me. Go therefore and make disciples of all nations, baptizing them in the name of the Father and of the Son and of the Holy Spirit, teaching them to observe all that I have commanded you. And behold, I am with you always, to the end of the age." (Matt. 28:18–20)

This passage is often called "the Great Commission." Jesus's commands are clear. He tells the disciples *what to do*, *where to do it*, and *how to do it*.

What to do. The disciples must go, make disciples, baptize, and teach. Grammatically, "make disciples" (v. 19) is the main verb. The other verbs—*go*, *baptizing*, and *teaching*—describe how the disciples are to accomplish that central task of disciple-making. They must *go* to share the good news of peace with God available by faith in Christ. As people repent of their sins and believe this good news, the disciples must *baptize* the new believers upon their profession of faith. Then the disciples need to *teach* these new disciples what Jesus first taught them.

Where to do it. Jesus instructs his followers to make disciples of "*all* nations" (v. 19). In other words, the scope of the mission extends to every corner of the earth. The word for *nations* in Greek (the original language of the New Testament) is *ethne*. This word doesn't refer to political nations like Turkey, China, or the United States, but smaller groups—the *ethnicities* of the world. This word also reveals God's purposes in redemption: he's drawing to himself worshipers among all the different people groups of the earth. In the Old Testament, God promised Abraham that all the families of the earth would be blessed through his seed (Gen. 12:1–3). He taught the nation of Israel to pray for the nations (Psalm 67). Now Jesus launches a global campaign to bring the kingdom of God to every people group, fulfilling the Abrahamic promise. At the end of history, we'll witness Christ's victorious enterprise as men and women from every tribe, tongue, and nation bow before the Messiah as worshipers of the one true God (Rev. 5:9).

How to do it. Notice Jesus brackets his command to the disciples with promises of his power and his presence. On the front end, Christ is the one with all authority in heaven and earth (Matt. 28:18). He has the authority as the divine Son of God to send us on heaven's mission. He has the authority to demand the allegiance of the peoples. On the back end, Christ promises that he will not leave us to our own devices. He will be with us always, to the end of the age (v. 20). These promises should make all the difference for people like you and me who struggle to be faithful to this Great Commission. Though we may feel overwhelmed— lacking wisdom and lacking strength—we only need to lean on Jesus who is with us now and always.

These disciples were given a worldwide task. But what are the implications? Must every Christian become a full-time missionary? If not, what role do non-missionaries play in the Great Commission?

Well, even these earliest disciples teach us that we all have different roles to play in carrying out Christ's commission. Some, like James, stayed primarily in Jerusalem to help build the church in that city. Others, like Peter and Philip, served farther away in other cities. Still others traveled far away. For example, church historians tell us that Thomas established Christian communities all the way in modern-day India.

Some stay and some go, but all own the mission and play their parts according to their various stations in life. Our responsibilities may be different, but the goal is the same. What a profound truth! Wherever God has you, you're not called simply to be a disciple but also to make disciples. God calls you to spread his gospel in your own community, and, even if you never leave the city where you were born, you still have a role to play in advancing the gospel to every nation.

Of course, at this point you might be thinking, *Really? I'm kind of an unlikely candidate for anything related to missions.* But let's take a moment to consider the types of people God uses to carry out the Great Commission.

Unlikely Participants

When I was in college, my favorite board game was Risk. If you've never played it, Risk is basically a map of the world broken into geographic areas that players try to conquer through higher dice rolls than their opponents. I liked the game because it allowed endless strategizing based on the perceived strength and intentions of opponents. You should only make a move to expand your territory if you have the strength to do so. Otherwise, your global plans come crashing down around you.

By all outward appearances, Jesus's plan to advance a global kingdom probably didn't look or sound strategic to his early followers. Even with the promises of his power and presence, his disciples might have looked around at each other and thought, "This is it? Shouldn't there be others more capable, more devoted, or less prone to failure?" When we start to think about

God's purpose to use us in his mission, we understand the words of the apostle Paul, "Who is equal to such a task?" (2 Cor. 2:16 NIV).

The book of Acts, of course, records that these weak and doubting men were transformed by the power of the Holy Spirit to become incredible leaders, preachers, and missionaries. You still might protest, "But I'm no Peter or Barnabas or Paul! Can God really use someone like me? What do I have to offer anyway?"

And yet, as we read about the growth of the church in Acts, we find that God not only used leaders like Peter, Barnabas, and Paul, he also used ordinary people—Christian converts from all walks of life who made it their ambition to follow Jesus. For every "full-time missionary" we read about, it seems there were many "ordinary" Christians involved in the task of spreading the good news. Check out these examples:

- The fellowship of the whole Jerusalem church leads to God adding "to their number day by day those who are being saved" (Acts 2:47).

- The Christians scattered (and forced to relocate) by the persecution in Jerusalem are all described as going "about preaching the word" (Acts 8:4).
- Ananias, simply described as "a disciple," is directed by God to go and share the good news with the future apostle Paul (Acts 9:10–12).
- God uses "men of Cyprus and Cyrene" who are scattered because of persecution to plant a church in the Greek-speaking city of Antioch (Acts 11:19–21).
- The church of Antioch sends and financially supports Paul on his first missionary journey, bringing him back for a missionary report afterward (Acts 13:1–3; 14:26–28).
- A church in Philippi is begun by a converted businesswoman named Lydia (Acts 16:14–15).
- A businessman and woman named Aquila and Priscilla help Paul with employment, become his traveling companions, and assist with church planting in Corinth and Ephesus (Acts 18:2–3, 18, 26).

- Some people like Mnason gave housing to traveling missionaries or provided space for churches to meet (Acts 21:16).

We could add to this list the names of many mentioned in the New Testament who seem to have been a part of different evangelistic efforts for a time—sometimes traveling with missionaries and other times staying to help a church get established. All of these people played a role in the spread of the early church. At the end of the book of Romans, for example, Paul names thirty-five people who would have been known to the church there and were a part of his missionary effort (Romans 16).

Many of these people would have been surprised if told that their names would end up in Scripture as a part of the record of missionary expansion. Each was simply a recipient of God's grace who desired to extend it to others. They were just ordinary church members, faithfully ministering in their local context. They could say as Paul did, "By the grace of God I am what

I am, and his grace to me was not without effect" (1 Cor. 15:10 NIV). It is the same thing that any of us can say if we have believed the gospel of Jesus and been adopted into his family. As unlikely as it might be that we are redeemed, and even more unlikely that God would see fit to use us in his plan of redemption—it is nonetheless true.

While we don't deserve to be used in God's mission, it's a great privilege. The God who makes no mistakes has chosen to use us!

But how? What can *you* do to support international missions where you are now? Let me suggest nine ways to be part of God's global mission.

Nine Ways to Participate in God's Global Mission

1. Know the Gospel

> For I delivered to you as of first importance what I also received: that Christ died for our sins according to the Scriptures. (1 Cor. 15:3 NIV)

In the business world, leaders talk about the idea of "mission drift"—when a company loses a clear sense of the main thing they are trying to do. As believers, if we aren't clear on our mission, we're likely to wander from it. Missions is about sharing the gospel, and the gospel is the good news that there is a way for lost and condemned people to find pardon and forgiveness in Jesus Christ.

At this point, many ask: "Isn't missions about more than that? What about life transformation, reconciling families, and changing cultures? What about social transformation?" Certainly making disciples includes teaching everything Jesus commands, which means individuals and even societies will be transformed. People who find forgiveness in Christ are changed and can say with the apostle Paul that God's "grace to me was not without effect" (1 Cor. 15:10 NIV). Beyond this, we certainly hope that larger transformations might follow. Often God works great changes in families and cultures through the work of missions. Throughout history, Christians have built schools, established hospitals, fed the poor, and cultivated community structures that have helped people flourish. But those larger social goods are not *the aim* of Christian missions, as if knowing Jesus is merely the means to more important social goods. Christ commissioned us to preach the gospel, calling sinners to repentance. We must "make disciples." In fact, sometimes, faithful preaching may mean communicating the gospel with no immediate, discernible effect at all.

At the root of our commission to make disciples of all nations is a call to share the good news of Jesus Christ. Because of this, it's essential that we know and articulate that message clearly.

As a pastor, I'm often conversing with new people who are in the process of joining our church. One of the things I ask them when we have a chance to sit down and talk is to explain what they understand the gospel to be. I simply ask, "What is the good news of Jesus Christ?" Many people get a little nervous when asked that question by a pastor, so I give them lots of grace as they put their answers into words. But ultimately I'm hoping that they can hit the high points of the gospel narrative: God, Man, Christ, Response.

God: God made the world; he is the King of creation. As our Creator, he is holy, just, loving, and good.

Man: Humankind was created in the image of God. Sadly, our first parents, Adam and Eve, chose to sin against God by disobeying him. All of us are likewise sinful in our actions and our attitudes. Our sinfulness leaves us under the just condemnation of a holy God. If left in this state, we will experience the eternal judgment of God in hell.

Christ: But God, because of his great love, made a way of salvation for sinful humanity. He sent Jesus Christ, his one and only Son, to become a man and rescue us from his own wrath. Jesus lived a perfectly righteous life, fulfilling all the commands of God. He never sinned. He died on a Roman cross as a payment for his people's sin. On the cross, Jesus took the judgment of God that you and I deserve. But on the third day, he rose from the dead. His resurrection is proof that the gospel is true, and our only hope for eternal life is found through him.

Response: This wonderful news about Jesus leaves every human being with a choice. We can continue in our sin awaiting the judgment of God, or we can turn away from our sin and believe in who Jesus is and what he did on the cross. If we turn to Christ, we have his promise that we will be pardoned, forgiven, and adopted into his family eternally.

I've rehearsed this gospel outline not just to give you something to memorize—though it wouldn't be a bad idea—but to encourage you to grow in your own understanding of the good news so that you can be an effective minister to others. Reminding ourselves of the centrality of the gospel keeps us from being sidetracked by less important issues. Even more, the better we know the gospel the more easily we will find it rolling off our tongues.[3]

2. Study Missions

> [Study] to present yourself to God as one approved, a worker who does not need to be ashamed and who correctly handles the word of truth. (2 Tim. 2:15 NIV)

Paul's command in 2 Timothy 2 specifically applies to pastors. But the principle remains true for all aspects of ministry. If we're going to be effective in supporting the work of missions, then we should study the work of missions.

Study missions and consider how God has carried out his global purpose of redemption. Perhaps the best way to do this is to meditate on the biblical storyline as it takes us from creation to new creation, unfolding the progress of God's saving grace to every nation of the earth.

Study God's promises to Abraham in Genesis 12 where God commits to bless all the nations of the earth. Familiarize yourself with the Old Testament examples where God used Israel to bring salvation to the Gentiles—stories of people such as Rahab, the Queen of Sheba, and the people of Nineveh. Read through the Gospel of Matthew and notice how Jesus includes Gentiles as part of his kingdom—a point that ultimately culminates in the Great Commission (Matt. 28:18–20). Study the growth of the early church in Acts, and notice how God brings Acts 1:8 to fruition as the gospel is made known "in Jerusalem and in all Judea and Samaria, and to the end of the earth" (Acts 1:8). Meditate on the heavenly visions in Revelation 5:9 and 7:9, where a great multitude from every tribe, people, language, and nation stands before the throne of God worshiping the Lamb.

Furthermore, read about the history of missions. Missionary biographies are a great way to ignite your love for missions. Here is my totally subjective "Top Ten" list of favorite missionary biographies:

- *To the Golden Shore: The Life of Adoniram Judson* by Courtney Anderson (1956): Judson was the first American foreign missionary, and he served for more than forty years in Burma.

- *Faithful Witness: The Life and Mission of William Carey* by Timothy George (1991): Carey, "The Father of Modern Missions," sparked a missions movement through his conviction that we are to use "means" to seek the conversion of the lost.

- *The Life and Diary of David Brainerd* edited by Jonathan Edwards (1749): This book is an honest depiction of the trials of missionary life. It's perhaps the most influential missionary biography of all time.

- *Shadow of the Almighty: The Life and Testament of Jim Elliot* by his wife, Elisabeth Elliot (1958): Jim Elliot said, "Take these idle sticks of my life, and let them burn for thee." He lived and died under this prayer among the tribes of Ecuador.

- *A Chance to Die: The Life and Legacy of Amy Carmichael* by Elisabeth Elliot (1987): Amy Carmichael modeled an unforgettable commitment to ministering to the poor in Donavur, India.

- *John G. Paton: Missionary to the New Hebrides*, an autobiography (1889): Cannibal headhunters wouldn't deter this hero of the faith.

- *J. Hudson Taylor: A Man in Christ* by Roger Steer (1990): Taylor was the founder of the China Inland Mission, and he persevered at sharing the gospel in China against incredible odds.

- *The Triumph of John and Betty Stam* by Geraldine Taylor (1935). This is a moving tribute to two Christians (aged twenty-seven and twenty-eight) who lost their lives in the turmoil of 1930s China.

- *For the Glory: The Untold and Inspiring Story of Eric Liddell, Hero of* Chariots of Fire by Duncan Hamilton (2017): This is the fascinating life story of an Olympic champion whose greatest ambition was to preach the gospel.

- *Mountain Rain: A Biography of James O. Fraser* by Eileen Crossman (1982): Fraser once said, "It has always been my dream for me to be on one donkey, my wife on a second, and all our worldly goods on a third." He lived in this way to reach the Lisu people of Southwest China.

3. Share the Gospel with Your Family, Friends, and Neighbors

> Therefore, we are ambassadors for Christ, God making his appeal through us. We implore you on behalf of Christ, be reconciled to God. (2 Cor. 5:20)

Another way to support missions is to evangelize the lost around you. On one hand, talking about Jesus should come naturally to every Christian. What a joy it should be to share with others the good news of how he has changed our lives! On the other hand, all of us struggle with the fear of man. None of us are as faithful as we could be at taking risks to talk about the gospel with those who are lost.

Paul describes unbelievers as those whom Satan has blinded (2 Cor. 4:4). Often, unbelievers will not understand the gospel. Sometimes they may even be hostile to it. Our great hope, however, is that the God who said "let light shine out of darkness" (2 Cor. 4:6) will shine in their hearts to bring about spiritual life and faith. Let's pray that God will use us as his instruments to help those around us come to know him!

If you're reading this book, then I assume you want to support international missions. But you can't be faithful in big things until you're faithful in little things. As you seek to find ways to be more involved supporting the progress of the gospel overseas, ask yourself: "How involved am I in evangelism right where I am?" The more invested you are in seeing the gospel go forward in your own community, the more capable you'll be at supporting that same work somewhere else in the world. As Jesus said, "One who is faithful in a very little is also faithful in much" (Luke 16:10). Pray and ask that God would make you bolder in gospel conversations with those around you. Pray specifically for the non-Christians you know. Our prayers often lead to conversations, and conversations lead to fruitfulness in ministry.

4. Invest in the Ministry of Your Local Church

> And they devoted themselves to the apostles'
> teaching and the fellowship, to the breaking
> of bread and the prayers. (Acts 2:42)

According to the New Testament, the Christian
life should be focused around the local church.
The New Testament never conceives of the idea
that a solitary, individual Christian might roam
free, detached from any meaningful connection
to the people of God. Instead, the teachings of
Jesus and the apostles regularly emphasize that
the Christian life should be characterized by a
commitment to the "one another" commands—
commands we can only fulfill in a local community of believers. We must love one another
(Rom. 12:10), serve one another (Gal. 5:13), be
kind to one another (Eph. 4:32), encourage one
another (1 Thess. 5:11), and stir up one another
to love and good works (Heb. 10:24). Even more,
Jesus connects ministry fruitfulness with the
quality of our community: "By this all people
will know that you are my disciples, if you have
love for one another" (John 13:35). Ultimately,

the only institution Jesus promises to build is the church (Matt. 16:18).

Of course, I'm not suggesting that there aren't wonderful parachurch ministries to get involved in or that we can't have any meaningful contribution to the kingdom as individuals. But I am suggesting that the Bible teaches that the primary way we should think about engaging in ministry is in and through the local church.

There are many practical ways to minister in your church:

- As you share the gospel with friends and neighbors, invite them to your church. Introduce them to other brothers and sisters in Christ who may be able to complement and augment your ministry to them.
- Make the prayer meetings of your local church a priority. Praying together with others about gospel outreach multiplies your own efforts.
- Get to know the ministries and missionaries that your church supports. You may have a unique role to play in encouraging a supported worker somewhere in the world by communi-

cating with them while they are on the mission field or blessing them with your friendship when they are on furlough.

- Remember that by investing in your local church, you are investing in the bride of Christ. You may only live somewhere for a few years, but by channeling your efforts in the local church your impact may continue well beyond.

5. Pray

> You also must help us by prayer. (2 Cor. 1:11)

Paul was convinced that prayer fueled, sustained, and prospered the work of missions. Missionary prayer letters are a gold mine of spiritual opportunity. Pray for the requests they name—the upcoming events, the current needs, and the pressing struggles. Beyond that, pray that the missionaries would be faithful to the Lord in their own personal holiness, their gospel outreach, and their persevering labor. Family devotions are enlivened by prayer for

missionaries. Church prayer meetings take on
new life by embracing the front lines of battle
in missionary work. Beginning by praying indi-
cates that we believe this is God's work, not ours.

6. *Give*

> I am well supplied, having received from
> Epaphroditus the gifts you sent. (Phil. 4:18)

Christian missions have always been supported by Christian giving. Jesus and the
disciples received support from women who
"provided for them out of their means" (Luke
8:3). Paul and his missionary bands were supported by churches and individuals. Giving to
missions is a powerful and wonderful thing
for Christians to do. It allows us to declare our
independence from the love of money, and to
declare our belief in things that are of eternal
value. Additionally, God takes joy when we
give the right way: he loves "a cheerful giver"
(2 Cor. 9:7).

Practically, how should this work? First, the
lion's share of your giving should go to your

church.[4] One practical benefit of giving to your
local church is that a church with godly elders
likely already has a wise, biblical, and effective
missions strategy. Our giving to the church
should reflect our trust that God is working
through these men who are set apart for this
task.

After we've given to the church, we should
seek out other ways we can give to strategic
and faithful missionary endeavors. All of our
resources are the Lord's, so when we find ourselves with surplus, we should ask what he wants
us to do with it. If he points us toward missions
work that we trust, we should seek to funnel our
resources in that direction.

Let me conclude this point with one important piece of advice: rather than spreading
small bits of money out to many missions efforts, it may be wiser to invest your giving in
just one or a few missionaries. By focusing on
just a few specific missionaries, you'll be able to
cultivate a more meaningful relationship with
those workers and ministries, and you'll be able
to focus your prayers on them as well. As you

do, remind yourself that the best investments are in things of eternal value.

7. Go

> Come over to Macedonia and help us.
> (Acts 16:9)

As I've said, not everyone is called to leave their home to take the gospel to a foreign place. Jesus's entire ministry happened within a hundred miles of the place he was born. James, one of the twelve apostles, remained a pastor in the Jerusalem church seemingly until his death (Acts 12:2).

At the same time, God often calls people to move somewhere else for the sake of the gospel. We should never shy away from asking the Lord, "Where do you want me to serve you?" Some of you reading this book may sense the Lord leading you to consider moving somewhere more in need of gospel work.

If you're sensing a desire to move to some place with gospel ministry needs, it's imperative that you remember the importance of your local church while making this decision. Your friends and the leaders of your church have an important role to play in praying for you, advising you, and equipping you for ministry ahead. This is how you can link an "internal sense of calling" with an "external affirmation of calling."

For others of us, perhaps the Lord is calling us to be involved in short-term missions opportunities. There may be mission trips organized by your local church to support the work of missionaries on the field. We should be careful as we evaluate these opportunities. "Missionary tourism" is not useful to anyone, and the goal is not to find a trip to a place you've always wanted to visit. The goal of short-term missions is to support the work of long-term missionaries. Consider how your short-term team could engage in serving missionaries—perhaps by engaging in evangelism in communities surrounding their church, perhaps by providing childcare for a conference that equips and refreshes missionaries, perhaps by bringing medical or engineering expertise to a work that needs it. These are just a few practical ways short-term missionaries can encourage long-term missionaries; there are many more.

One last category of "go" that we should consider connects with your current profession. In an increasingly global economy, there may be opportunities for you to remain in the same or a similar job but to do it in a place strategic for the gospel. For instance, if you're an engineer in Nebraska, why not consider looking for engineering jobs in an international context near missionaries you know and trust? By moving there and connecting with a local church, you may be able to have a significant impact on gospel work in that region.

8. Inform

> We want you to know, brothers, about the grace of God that has been given among the churches. (2 Cor. 8:1)

As you become more informed about the work of missions, take the time to inform others! Certainly pastors should be informed about the work and lives of missionaries that the church supports, but laypeople are often more effective at spreading good information from member to member. I have been friends for years with members of my home church who model this well. They regularly stay in contact with us when we are on the field, writing emails and calling us to find out about our needs. They've been on several short-term trips to support our work. When we're on furlough, they're the first people to want to host us in their homes.

Not surprisingly, they're also some of the best "spreaders" of missions information among the congregation. In recent years, they've hosted "missions nights" in their homes to pray for missionaries and learn more about what God is doing around the world. As you get more interested and excited about international missions, take seriously the work of letting others learn more along with you.

9. Mobilize

Therefore we ought to support people like these, that we may be fellow workers for the truth. (3 John 8)

"Fellow worker" is not a church office like elder or deacon, but it's nevertheless a phrase you will find throughout the New Testament. Paul is constantly greeting his fellow workers, sending his fellow workers, and encouraging fellow workers. In 3 John 8, John tells the church that we ought to financially support missionaries so that we can be fellow workers together for the truth of the gospel. The ministry of the apostles was not only one of raising up more believers through the preaching of the gospel but of raising up more leaders who could join them in the work.

How can you catalyze others to support the work of international missions? Consider bringing a fellow church member along to a meal you are hosting for international students. Invite someone to join you on a short-term mission trip. Help a leader from another church learn about how they could join your church's efforts to support missions in another part of the world.

Maybe you could begin praying now that God would use you to mobilize more fellow workers for the task of missions!

The Glory of the Impossible

Samuel Zwemer spent thirty-eight years serving in Arabia and Egypt. He wrote movingly of the work of ministry in what he called "pioneer missions":

> The unoccupied fields of the world await those who are willing to be lonely for the sake of Christ. To the pioneer missionary, the words of our Lord Jesus Christ to the apostles when He showed them His hands and His feet, come with special force: "As my Father hath sent Me, even so send I you" (John 20:21). He came into the world, and it was a great unoccupied mission field. "He came unto His own, and His own received Him not" (John 1:11). He came and His welcome was derision, His life, suffering, and His throne, the Cross.
>
> As He came, He expects us to go. We must follow in His footprints. The pioneer missionary, in overcoming obstacles and difficulties . . . has the privilege not only

of knowing Christ and the power of His resurrection, but also something of the fellowship of His suffering. For the people of Tibet or Somaliland, Mongolia or Afghanistan, Arabia or Nepal, the Sudan or Abyssinia, he may be called to say with Paul, "Now I rejoice in my sufferings for you and fill to the brim the penury of the afflictions of Christ in my flesh for His body's sake which is the Church" (Col. 1:24).

What is it but the glory of the impossible! Who would naturally prefer to leave the warmth and comfort of hearth and home and the love of the family circle to go after a lost sheep, whose cry we have faintly heard in the howling of the tempest? Yet such is the glory of the task that neither home-ties nor home needs can hold back those who have caught the vision and the spirit of the Great Shepherd. Because the lost ones are His sheep, and He has made us His shepherds and not His hirelings, we must bring them back.

"Although the road be rough and steep
I go to the desert to find my sheep."[5]

I read these words as a twenty-two-year-old,
and they helped lead me to the mission field
where I've happily served for many years. They
still resonate with me, but the same zeal for
God's glory and the return of his lost sheep is
something that needs to be spread far beyond
"the pioneer missionary."

My hope is that this short book has convinced you that the "unoccupied fields of the
world" call you to action right where you are.
The "glory of the impossible" doesn't begin with
the stuff of *Foxe's Book of Martyrs* or your favorite missionary biography. It begins with faithfulness in the little things of your life—little things
that our Lord is often pleased to use in big ways.
As we embrace our calling to be his disciples and
to be involved in making disciples of all nations,
we discover the joy of living the way our Savior
lived, as a good and faithful servant of others.
May God be pleased to use our efforts for our
good and his glory for all the nations.

Notes

1. Personal stories involving other individuals are shared in this booklet with permission from those individuals. Sometimes pseudonyms have been used for privacy.
2. Elisabeth Elliot, *Shadow of the Almighty: The Life and Testament of Jim Elliot* (New York: Harper & Brothers, 1958), 108.
3. A great book to deepen your understanding of the good news is Greg Gilbert, *What Is the Gospel?* (Wheaton, IL: Crossway, 2010).
4. For more on this point see Jamie Dunlop, *Why Should I Give to My Church?* (Wheaton, IL: Crossway, 2021).
5. Samuel Zwemer, *The Unoccupied Mission Fields of Africa and Asia* (Marshall Brothers Ltd., London: 1911), 221–22. Scripture quoted in this excerpt are from the King James Version of the Bible. Public domain.

Scripture Index

IX 9Marks

Building Healthy Churches

9Marks exists to equip church leaders with a biblical vision and practical resources for displaying God's glory to the nations through healthy churches.

To that end, we want to see churches characterized by these nine marks of health:

1. Expositional Preaching
2. Gospel Doctrine
3. A Biblical Understanding of Conversion and Evangelism
4. Biblical Church Membership
5. Biblical Church Discipline
6. A Biblical Concern for Discipleship and Growth
7. Biblical Church Leadership
8. A Biblical Understanding of the Practice of Prayer
9. A Biblical Understanding and Practice of Missions

Find all our Crossway titles and other resources at 9Marks.org.

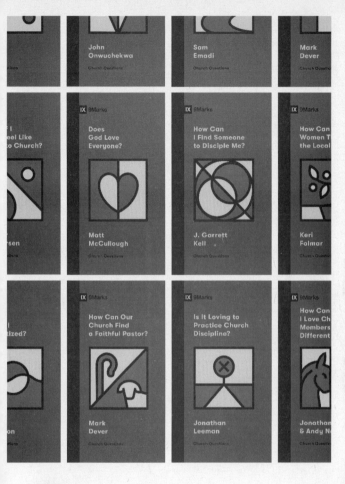

IX 9Marks Church Questions

Providing ordinary Christians with sound and
accessible biblical teaching by answering
common questions about church life.

For more information, visit crossway.org.